7 MYTHS AND SEVEN TRICKS IN NINE STEPS::

The truth & tricks about
learning course product creation
that THEY don't know

By
Paul Benson & Glen Ford

Published By

Mississauga, Canada

Sale of this book without a cover may be unauthorized. If this book is without a cover it may have been reported as unsold and destroyed. Neither the publisher nor the author will have been paid for their efforts.

© First Edition 2010, Paul Benson, Glen Ford and TrainingNOW
© Second Edition 2013, Paul Benson, Glen Ford and TrainingNOW

All rights reserved. No part of this book may be reproduced in any form or by any means without written permission by the publisher. If purchased in electronic form, the purchaser may make a reasonable number of copies for personal use as backup or to view on alternative media. The creation of copies for lending or resale is forbidden.

Published by TrainingNOW, Mississauga & Oakville, Ontario, Canada
http://www.TrainingNOW.ca
http://www.LearningCreators.com
http://www.LearningCreators.ca

Limit of Liability/Disclaimer of warranty: While the publisher and author have used their best efforts in preparing this book, they make no representations or warranties with respect to the accuracy or completeness of the contents of this book and specifically disclaim any implied warrantees of merchantability or fitness for a particular purpose. No warranty may be created or extended by sales representatives or written sales materials. The advice and strategies contained herein may not be suitable for your situation. You should consult with a professional where appropriate. Neither the publisher nor author shall be liable for any loss of profit or any other commercial damages, including but not limited to special, incidental, consequential or other damages.

R20131127.112600

To our families,
they make writing books possible

And

To our readers,
who make it worthwhile

For More Books On Similar Topics
http://www.trainingnow.ca
For More Information On This And Related Topics
http://www.learningcreators.com/blog

TrainingNOW Books By Glen Ford

How to Write Your Own How-To EBook in 24 Hours or Less: The information products secret revealed!

How to Document a Project Plan: What you need to know to design a project management plan quickly and easily

How to Blog for Money: 9 strategies to get your blog earning money online and off

Writer's Block Demolition: Finding the time to write, keeping writing, and finish YOUR book

101 Writing Tweets: 101 tips and tweets about writing how-to books for the Kindle

As Glen Douglas

How To Build A Raised Garden Bed

With Paul Benson

101 Limericks About Public Speaking

7 Myths and Seven Tricks in Nine Steps: The truth & tricks about learning course product creation that THEY don't know

Most books are available in both Kindle and Print versions.

Table of Contents

CHAPTER 1: WELL WHAT WOULD YOU EXPECT FROM AN INDUSTRY THAT CAN'T IDENTIFY ITS PRODUCT?   1

CHAPTER 2: THE SEVEN DEADLY MYTHS OF INFORMATION PRODUCT CREATION   9

MYTH NUMBER 1: PRODUCT CREATION IS EASY, MARKETING IS HARD   11
MYTH NUMBER 2: YOU SHOULD START BY SELLING PLR PRODUCTS.   14
MYTH NUMBER 3: REPURPOSING IS THE EASY WAY TO CREATE PRODUCTS   17
MYTH NUMBER 4: PRODUCT QUALITY DOESN'T MATTER ONLY CONTENT   19
MYTH NUMBER 5: CREATING IN ONE MEDIA IS EASIER THAN ANOTHER   20
MYTH NUMBER 6: BUILD IT AND THEY WILL COME   22
MYTH NUMBER 7: ANY PRODUCT CREATION SYSTEM WILL WORK   24

CHAPTER 3: THE SEVEN DEADLY MYTHS OF KINDLE PUBLISHING   27

MYTH NUMBER 1: START BY PUBLISHING OUT-OF-COPYRIGHT OR PLR BOOKS   28
MYTH NUMBER 2: GET SOMEONE TO WRITE A BOOK FOR $50 AND SELL IT FOR A MILLION   30
MYTH NUMBER 3: YOU WILL GET RICH WRITING A BOOK   33
MYTH NUMBER 4: PEOPLE DON'T WANT PAPER BOOKS   36
MYTH NUMBER 5: AMAZON WILL DO ALL YOUR MARKETING FOR YOU   38
MYTH NUMBER 6: SET IT AND WALK AWAY, MONEY IS GENERATED FOREVER   39
MYTH NUMBER 7: GIVING AWAY YOUR BOOKS WILL GET YOU SALES   42

CHAPTER 4: THE SEVEN TRICKS OF INFORMATION PRODUCT CREATION   45

TRICK NUMBER 1: KNOW YOUR AUDIENCE BEFORE YOU START   47
TRICK NUMBER 2: SUCCESS BEGINS WITH THE RIGHT SYSTEM   49
TRICK NUMBER 3: DO STRUCTURAL POLISHING BEFORE THE HEAVY WORK   50
TRICK NUMBER 4: USE TOOLS THAT WORK WITH YOU NOT AGAINST YOU   53
TRICK NUMBER 5: IT'S EASIER TO COPY THAN TO CREATE   55

TRICK NUMBER 6: POOR CONTENT THIEVES GET CAUGHT. GOOD ONES REPURPOSE RIGHT.	57
TRICK NUMBER 7: USE OVERHEADS EFFECTIVELY & EFFICIENTLY	61

CHAPTER 5: THE BENEFITS OF AN INFORMATION PRODUCT CREATION SYSTEM AND WHY YOUR BUSINESS IS AT RISK WITHOUT ONE — 65

WHY USE A SYSTEM?	66
WHAT'S IN AN INFORMATION PRODUCT CREATION SYSTEM?	68
WHAT ARE THOSE STEPS, TASKS, ETC…?	68
RESEARCHING FOR THE NEW PRODUCT	69
PRE-PLANNING	70
PLANNING THE NEW PRODUCT	72
DESIGNING THE NEW PRODUCT	73
STRUCTURAL EDITING	75
CONTENT CREATION	76
EDITING	78
PUBLISHING THE PRODUCT	79
GETTING THE BEST FROM YOUR INFORMATION PRODUCT CREATION SYSTEM	81

CHAPTER 6: CONCLUSION — 83

A NOTE FROM THE AUTHORS — 85

WHO WE ARE — 87

Chapter 1: Well what would you expect from an industry that can't identify its product?

> *"Those who can't do, teach. And those who can't teach, manage. And those who can't manage, criticize."*
>
> - An Anonymous wag.

It doesn't take long for anyone to realize that there are a few problems with internet marketing. Especially with that part of the market that deals with selling advice and teaching others how to do stuff.

After all, any industry, which has such a hard time identifying what its product is, has to have a few problems!

And the "guru" industry certainly does fit that bill.

What is the "guru" industry?

It's the expert industry. Or as one industry guru calls it ... the advice business.

It is an industry that exists to teach people how to do any number of different things. Whether it's running a business, or losing weight. Fixing your bike or fixing your finances. Whether it's designing a garden or designing a dress. It's an industry that is focused on helping people to grow through learning.

And it is an industry that has exploded with the growth of the internet.

Usually it calls itself the information products business. But that's not true. Yes, it provides information. But the people who named it "information products" were showing their own prejudices and lack of knowledge. They came from the information products industry and they saw the complimentary parts. So they figured it was part of their industry. So the industry was called the information products business.

But the real information products business is much bigger. And it tends to have a slightly different focus. More of a computer and data manipulation and retrieval bias than the information sharing of this business.

So information products is a bad description.

It used to be called the education industry or teaching. But that's also a pretty large field and it tends to be focused on a demographic that most of us in this industry don't care about. The old name of adult education or adult training is at least closer but it's still not quite right.

You see this industry includes training, coaching and consulting.

It's the internet marketing business and it really is the advice business when you get to its basic realities.

It's an industry which teaches anything to anybody and gives any type of advice to anyone who'll listen.

Its product is learning content.

What is learning content? It's the information contained in any learning event ... training, coaching or consulting. It's the systems, skills and intelligence that are being taught.

But it doesn't just stop there.

Learning content needs to be delivered. And it's delivered in many different media. It's delivered as a DVD set watched in the customer's home. Or it's delivered as a webinar participated in over the internet. Or a podcast. Or a teleseminar. Or a live seminar. Or a speech. Or even an eBook or traditional textbook.

The product creation cycle for this advice industry includes researching the product, converting the information into learning content, and then reformatting the learning content into a course or speech or event or coaching session or consultation in a media that is appropriate to the need.

Given all these media is it any wonder that people have problems separating the material or subject from the training materials, from the delivery media, and from the marketing media?

Making matters worse, the people who have accidently ended up in the industry don't usually have a background in the industry. So is it any wonder that the industry has developed a strong belief in myths?

You know myths ... those supposed truths that no one has bothered to question because they've been around since the start of the industry.

And is it any wonder that the industry has developed a set of tricks? Tricks are those shortcuts that help people survive from day to day. Especially when they are working in an area that is as complex as training.

And given the fact that so many of the participants are accidentally in the business or are marketers for the business, is it any wonder that many of the more vocal in the industry doesn't even realize that a system for developing the product has been developed? Not only developed but tested and been in use for many, many, many years. In fact, long before the internet was even possible!

It's true.

And given the fact that the Kindle eBook market (and the KOBO, Nook, and iBook markets) have grown astronomically is it any wonder that myths about the eBook publishing market have grown up just as quickly? After all in just ten short years, the eBooks have grown from just 0.05% of the market in 2002 to 41% in 2013. The Kindle publishing market as a source of revenue has been discovered. And myths about it have grown as "gurus" have entered the fray, dispensing advice willy-nilly.

In this book we'll share with you seven myths about this industry that you need to beware of. We'll also share seven myths about eBook publishing in particular. We'll share with you seven tricks you need to be aware of. And we'll explain the nine steps which the rest of the advice industry -- that part that's not on the internet -- has tested, used and improved. A system that is perfect for developing learning content (including eBooks) for the internet age.

Chapter 2: The seven deadly myths of information product creation

> *"Myth could be as sustaining as reality - sometimes even more so."*
>
> - Alexander McCall Smith,
> *The Lost Art of Gratitude*

Myths aren't just found in Greek and Roman history. They're alive and well in the world of the internet. And like any other information the internet seems to be able to spread and multiply myths like never before.

There are a lot of myths surrounding information products. But what do you expect? Even the name "information products" is incorrectly used. Information products is really a wide group of products including newspapers, news aggregators, publicity release distribution, software and a great many other types of information. Including most internet companies. Anyone who deals in the creation, aggregation, manipulation or transmission of information is in the "information products" industry. It's a big industry.

Most internet marketers aren't really selling generic information products. They're in the training field or the publishing industry or the consulting industry or a combination of training, consulting and publishing. In short they are really in the advice business. And yes, those are sort of, kind of in the information products industry -- if you ignore everything else that's also in the info business.

Is it any wonder that an industry that is so poorly understood by its participants is filled with myths?

The problem with myths is that despite the fact that they aren't true sometimes people believe them. And that can be disastrous. Both for those people who mistakenly believe the myths. And also for those who depend on those people.

Seven of the most deadly myths that internet marketers believe are:

1. Product creation is easy, marketing is hard
2. You should start by selling PLR products
3. Repurposing is the easy way to create products
4. Product quality doesn't matter only content
5. Creating in one media is easier than in another
6. Build it and they will come
7. Any product creation system will work

So let's get ready for a review of seven of the most disastrous myths.

Myth Number 1: Product creation is easy, marketing is hard

This myth says that anyone can create eBooks and videos. That everyone is able to teach.

But marketing must be hard because everyone is uncomfortable selling. So you really need to focus on learning how to market and the product creation process will just come naturally.

It's hard to blame this myth on any one group. Everyone seems to be to blame for this. At its root, the blame is really on the human condition. We all tend to overestimate the value of what we do. And underestimate the value of what another person does. And we also tend to automatically presume that because we can do something, we can teach it.

The truth is that all elements of a business must work together if a business is to succeed. It's the whole, the synergy that is important. Not any one part. No one part is more or less important than another. That's why small businesses can outsource key parts of their business successfully. And yet, large businesses often can't. It's precisely because small businesses are small, that outsourced pieces can be monitored after the outsourcing. Large business often toss out the monitoring staff with the bath water. They lose the ability to monitor the outsourced work.

On the other hand, it's also why many small businesses fail. The owner/manager forgets that their primary responsibility is to run the whole of the business. Instead they focus either on what they do well -- which is usually the product side. Or they focus on what they don't do well -- which is usually the marketing side. As for the administrative side ... not even administration types like to focus on that.

And of course, if we are learning how to do something (like marketing) it is always harder in our eyes to do it. So because most entrepreneurs aren't marketers they see marketing as the most important element. Even if they do tend to spend much of their time on producing the product or service they sell.

And teaching suffers from the same issue.

Teaching others how to do something is an entirely different skill from either doing or selling. And creating courses -- which is product creation in the advice business -- is yet another skill. If you are in the business of teaching, then teaching is a core skill you need to develop. Your courses are your product after all.

The truth is whatever you can do well is easy. Whatever you can't do well is hard. And all the functions are equally important.

Myth Number 2: You should start by selling PLR products.

Private Label Rights is the internet marketer's equivalent of rebranding hard goods like refrigerators. Grab someone else's product. Stick your name on it. Make lots of money easily, quickly and painlessly.

And like most get-rich-quick schemes it often fails miserably.

Private Labeling is a technique that has been used for generations in physical goods. Simply put, one company designs a product. But they have a limit to how much of that product they can sell. Other companies may decide to market a competing product but they have a limit on how much they are willing to spend to get that product. The solution is for the first company to create several variations of their product. Maybe with a different colored case. Or with slightly different functions. Or a few additional features. Or a few less. They then put the second company's logo on the product and the second company sells it.

This works well in the physical products world. The basic product is protected by patents. The manufacturer gets additional sales and reduced costs from volume. Both companies make extra profits and get extra sales without the additional costs. Everyone wins.

Unfortunately, the world of information is totally different. And the technique of relabeling just doesn't translate well.

First off, physical products are protected by patent law. These laws protect the underlying intellectual property while allowing for sales of the result. But training and publishing products (or some info products if you insist on the wrong name) are protected by copyright law. Those are two separate and different legal foundations. Which means that the rights which are protected (or not) are also different. Bottom line is that most of the rights you buy (and rely on) with private label rights sales, can't be bought or sold. They're moral rights. They belong to the author ... period!

Secondly, most PLR products are secondary products or obsolete products. They're past their principle life. And they were often created by less than perfect trainers in the first place. As a result they frequently contain outdated or incorrect information. Even things as simple as spelling errors can be found in PLR products.

That's not to say that all PLR products are bad. Or that they have no use at all. But they are not a substitute for a quality product developed specifically for you.

Myth Number 3: Repurposing is the easy way to create products

Don't write eBooks. Just put on a course and then have the audio transcribed into a book. It's much easier and gives just as good a set of results.

Or so they'd have you believe.

The biggest problem with this myth isn't that it makes new internet marketers underestimate the issues involved. It's that it takes a valid, valuable technique and undervalues it. It makes people think that repurposing is on the same level as using PLR products. And that's just not true.

Repurposing has its use.

Let me say that again. Repurposing is an important tool in the internet marketer's tool bag. It has its place and it needs to be done in that place. And done right.

For example, you can start with a book, and select sections out. Add a new opening and concluding paragraph and you have an article or blog entry. Take the points made in that article and use it to create a set of visuals (the proper term for slides or PowerPoint slides). Use the article as the script and you have the basis for a 5 minute video.

Or take the design of the book, move elements around and you have the design for a seminar. Then take the paragraphs out of the book and put them in to create a large part of the script for the course. Of course, you are still going to have a great deal of writing but you will be closer that having to completely reinvent the wheel.

The problem isn't that repurposing is a myth. It is a very useful technique. The problem is that most people are being sold on repurposing the wrong way and using it when it isn't right. Repurposing when done right is effective but not it is never easy. If it is easy then you probably aren't doing it right.

Myth Number 4: Product quality doesn't matter only content

This is one of the most frightening myths around. If you listen to some internet marketers they'll tell you that you can forget about quality if you just concentrate on content. Provide plenty of good content and your buyer will ignore any spelling or grammar mistakes or any poor camera techniques.

Funny thing is ... they're usually the ones who have mistakes all over their content!

Bit of self serving advice there, eh what?

Have you noticed that the best advice marketers – people like Tony Robbins – sell very professional looking products? That they spend a great deal of effort and money polishing the look of their product?

The frightening thing is that the myth is almost 180 degrees from the truth. Most of your readers won't know good content. That's why they're reading your eBook. They're hunting for a solution to their problem, a way to avoid something they fear or a way to achieve something they want. But in all cases they are reading your book because you have information they need. And simply put they can't judge your content because they don't have the information that would allow them to do so.

Instead, your audience judges your eBook or information product primarily based on the organization of the information, and the delivery of the information. That latter element translates as spelling and grammar for written materials and camera and speaking techniques for video and audio. Exactly what those gurus claim doesn't matter!

Myth Number 5: Creating in one media is easier than another

Every guru you talk to will tell you that their media is the easiest. Look around, are they into making videos? Then videos are much easier to make than webinars. Are they into slide shows? Then a webinar is the way to get your information across. Are they uncomfortable in front of the camera? Then podcasts and teleseminars are definitely the best.

EBooks are about the only version that no one seems to want to admit is better than the alternatives!

Guess what? The truth is that it doesn't matter. Each has advantages and each has disadvantages. If you're great in one you'll be great in another. At least as far as content goes. The only difference is what you are most comfortable with using. And that comfort is what most of us present as the quality of product in each media.

All the media take approximately the same amount of time to create. Why? Because all of them take about the same amount of effort to design and then turn into a package. And they all follow roughly the same process. Yes, there are differences in design from one media to the other and the order things are done, but the basic process is the same.

Where they differ is in how comfortable you are working with each of the media. For example, many people are deathly afraid of live seminars. Yet they are perfectly fine with a webinar. Or to pick an example that's close to my heart, they may be perfectly fine with live seminars but uncomfortable in front of a video camera! (Guess who? Nah, only one guess per customer! Trust me you don't need more than that. At least the camera didn't explode like I was afraid it would!)

Often this translates into knowing how to use the tools of the particular media. In writing being able to spell and write grammatically correct sentences is critical. In video it isn't. In audio being able to speak clearly and vary one's tone and volume to carry interest is critical. In writing not so much. Each of the media have different needs as far as presentation goes. But the effort and the content is surprising similar.

Myth Number 6: Build it and they will come

This myth has been cause of the destruction of more hi-tech businesses than any other. And business on the internet seems to have given it a new lease on life.

Yes, you can build a website to sell your eBook or videos or audios or home study kit. But that doesn't mean you'll actually manage to sell anything. In fact, it doesn't mean that you'll even get people visiting your site.

All products -- let me repeat that -- ALL PRODUCTS, need to be marketed in order to be successful. And that includes products on the internet. More so in fact for internet businesses.

There are four elements of marketing that you need to consider when you are looking to sell your courseware over the internet. First, you need to select a niche that has potential. Second, you need to consider the customer when you are creating your course. Third you need to create sales pages that touch the customer and motivate them to take action. These sales pages include an opt-in page as well as sales pages for the products themselves. And fourth, you need to drive traffic. How you drive traffic is a marketing decision. But without traffic no one will ever read your opt-in page or your sales page or buy your course!

Myth Number 7: Any product creation system will work

This myth seems to be most prevalent with writing eBooks as your media. Maybe because many of the other media pundits presume you can just create learning content without any system at all.

But it just ain't so!

In fact, you need to use a learning content creation system when creating courseware. Why? Because that's what people in the advice business do when they aren't providing direct advice in the form of coaching or consulting ... they create courseware. Learning content is just another name for courseware with a bit of philosophy thrown in. Actually learning content refers to courseware without getting bogged down in the media the course is delivered in. It doesn't matter if you're creating eBooks or webinars, videos or podcasts. If you're creating learning content you need a system to create it.

But why? Why not just get up there and write? Or get up on the stage and talk until your voice gives out?

The answer is simple -- complexity. As your courseware increases in complexity it becomes more and more difficult to organize. It becomes more difficult to make sense of the information. And it becomes more difficult to present the information in a quality manner.

Let's take the example of an eBook. If you are writing a blog post or an article you'll probably need to write about 300 to 500 words. In that number of words you can only write three or four paragraphs. Given that one of them is your introduction and another may be your conclusion, that doesn't leave a lot of room for information. In fact, you can only make one to two points in such an article. That doesn't represent much of a need for organization!

On the other hand, a 60 page eBook involves roughly 15,000 words or 150 paragraphs. That's at least, one hundred and fifty points that need to be selected and organized in order to make a common point and to teach a lesson. Needless to say a design process that works for an article won't be able to handle an eBook. And a design process that works for an eBook will be too much for an article. (By the way, this difference in the need for a design process applies to 2 minute marketing videos and 3 hour training videos as well.)

Chapter 3: The seven deadly myths of kindle publishing

> *"Anyone who believes what a cat tells him deserves all he gets.*
>
> - Neil Gaiman,
> *Stardust*

It was inevitable that the Internet Marketing "gurus" would discover publishing on the Kindle as an opportunity both to make money themselves and to relieve the uninitiated of their money.

It hasn't taken long for a new set of myths to arise about this new channel.

1. Start by publishing out-of-copyright or PLR books
2. Get someone to write a book for $50 and sell it for a million
3. You will get rich writing a book
4. People don't want paper books
5. Amazon will do all your marketing for you
6. Set it and walk away, money is generated forever
7. Giving away your books will get you sales

So let's look a little deeper at these myths.

Myth Number 1: Start by publishing out-of-copyright or PLR books

One of the myths that keeps cropping up is that a good place to start publishing is by publishing out-of-copyright books and PLR books that you have kicking around. Nothing could be further from the truth.

The truth is that none of the booksellers want to carry books that are self-published but not yours. It isn't worth it to them.

PLR or Private Label Rebranded books as we've discussed before aren't actually legal under copyright laws. Using them not only opens your booksellers like Amazon up to legal exposure but the concept is flawed. If there are twenty people selling the same book under a different name, then the reading public is going to get upset. Why should they buy this stuff? I know that I've bought slightly changed version of books (usually the title and author are the major changes). Typically these books get thrown against a wall and then returned with a very nasty note. I'm Canadian. We're not supposed to get upset or vent our feelings. How do you think other more demonstrative readers act? And if readers get upset, Amazon and company will have no one to sell books to. So Amazon and the other booksellers react negatively to people who try to sell PLR books. In fact, they will ban you if you try to sell PLR books.

The same thing applies to a lesser extent with regard to copyright-free books. These are books whose author has died over 70 years before. First off, obviously these are old books, so they are under the difficulty of marketing what has been seen before and what may not be relevant. Secondly, many of the better books are available in a plethora of editions. So unless your edition is special – either because the book is rare and long out of print or because you have done something special to it – many of the booksellers will not carry your book.

So while the idea of reselling PLR and copyright-free books has merit (less so in the case of PLR), the reality is that Amazon and other booksellers don't want it. So you will have a hard time selling or even publishing those types of books. And you could easily find your account banned because you tried to sell them.

Myth Number 2: Get someone to write a book for $50 and sell it for a million

One of the realities of the modern world is that there is a great deal of variation in quality of life. And the cost of living. So can you get someone to write a book for $50 for you? Yes, you can.

However, the question is where do they need to live?

A 50-page book will take about a week for a person to write unless they are extremely prolific. If they are very prolific then they can crank it out in 5 days (actually 3 days to write and 2 days to recover). If they could produce one book per week (unlikely) then they potentially could earn the princely sum of $2,600 per year (unless they took a vacation).

Do you know anywhere in the English speaking world that people could survive on $2,600 per year?

A 50-page book written by a North American or British professional ghostwriter will cost between $2,000 and $15,000 depending on the professional credentials of the individual if there is no research involved. The simple truth is that the only way to get a book written for $50 is if it is: computer generated, ripped off, or written by non-English speakers. The majority of these books fit into one of the two latter categories.

If you try to publish a book that is plagiarized (i.e. ripped off), you are opening yourself up to a serious exposure. I can't emphasize that enough. **DO NOT DO IT!** It isn't worth it. Everyone in the publishing industry fears that form of theft called plagiarizing. They treat copyright as a sacred cow. The person holding the copyright will sue you. Amazon (and other booksellers) will cancel your account. And if you cross the line far enough you will find yourself blacklisted. Do not do it. After all, you wouldn't want your work stolen from you, would you?

Delivery is a key element in the quality equation for books and other learning content. Whenever a book is written by someone who doesn't speak the language natively, the quality of writing is questionable. If they are fluent, the phrasing is usually overly formal. If they aren't (and they won't be if they accept $1 a page when the going rate is $1 a word), then the grammar and spelling will always reflect their native language. It will be very obvious – in word choice and use – that they do not speak the language natively. That means you will need to edit the book before you can publish it.

While editing is part of the process of publishing, there are many types of editing. The typical light editing (sometimes called proofreading or proofing) can be had for as low as $5 per 250 word page. For a typical short book (50 pages) that means you will be spending around $250. However, in depth editing and rewriting (which is what most $50 books need) will cost at least 4 times that (or more). Meaning your $50 book just cost you $1050.

Of course, you could always just release the book as it stands. But could your reputation as a publisher stand the fallout? Most can't. And you'll find that your book will have a very short shelf-life as a result.

Myth Number 3: You will get rich writing a book

Do you know many rich writers? No, I didn't think so. In fact, it's possible that you can list the names of all the rich writers. There aren't that many. Amazon has recently admitted that only 12 self-published authors had sales of more than 100,000 books. In fact, only 50 authors around the world (traditional and otherwise) earned more than $80,000 on any book.

And yet, the internet marketers would have you believe that you can become a millionaire by writing a single book. Unfortunately, the numbers just don't support that.

The maximum price that an eBook can sell for on Amazon is $9.99 of which the author gets roughly 70% (there's a charge for bandwidth). Most books, however, sell for $3.99 or less. That means the author gets $6.75 at most but more likely $2.50 per book. In order to earn $50,000 per year you need to earn roughly $136 a day. That means you need 54 books sold per day at $3.99 or 20 books at $9.99.

To be a bestselling author on all the lists you only need 68 books per day. In fact, if you know how to scam the system you can be a bestselling author on even less. And remember that you need to do this consistently over a long period of time. Most books just don't last that long on the bestselling lists. Most last only a week at that rate. A great one will last ten. You need to do this day in, day out, year after year to make a reasonable salary of $50,000.

Do you really think you will be one of the top 100 authors out of the millions that are listed on Amazon?

Of course, it's not all doom and gloom. There is a way.

Traditionally, most writers did not make money until they reached 8 books. If each of your books sold just 2 books a day you'd make your required income level. Of course, traditional publishers cheated by reducing the amount of money they paid you but let's ignore that for the moment.

With Amazon's promotion schedule, the current requirement is for 12 books. This allows one book a week to be on promotion during each 3 month cycle. With each book selling copies of the other books, it is likely that the number of books sold will be much higher than the 1 or 2 books a day that is common.

That's how you make money with Kindle books. Have multiple books each contributing one weekend per 90 day cycle as a promotion (either free or countdown) and you'll have a consistent money machine. If each of your books produces only 4 books a day in sales on average, you'll make your target income. The more books, the more likely you are to make your target income.

And even if you don't make a full-time income, the income you do make will help pay your bills.

Myth Number 4: People don't want paper books

One of the myths you'll hear over and over is, "Write a short book and then sell it as a Kindle book because no one pays attention to how long the book is and no one wants paper books anymore." The truth is that roughly 60% of the books sold in 2013 were physical books. They produced roughly 80% of the total income.

Paper based books are still very important. People like holding the product in their hot little hands.

As a self-published author, physical books are critical for your income. In fact, I have books that routinely sell three to four times the number of physical books as they do eBooks. And I'm not unusual.

If you aren't producing a physical book, you are leaving money on the table.

The key here is that physical books need to be above a minimum length. Below 150 pages, they can't have a printed spine. Below 100 pages, they look like a pamphlet with a hard cover. In short, very short books look amateurish. The old standard of 50 pages being suitable just won't work in the physical world. And that means if you want 50 page specials, then you will give up roughly half your potential income.

Myth Number 5: Amazon will do all your marketing for you

Amazon is one of the biggest marketers on the planet, if it isn't the biggest. People go to Amazon to buy and Amazon will put your products in front of the customer. In short, in order to make their money they need to push your product.

The obvious leap in logic, therefore, is that if you leave your marketing to Amazon, you will still sell a ton of books. And it's a leap that seems to be a favorite of the internet gurus.

The problem is it's a leap that isn't justified.

Although Amazon is a virtual store for books and other items, they stock more than just your book. They may stock dozens, hundreds, or even thousands of books many of which are almost identical to yours. If you believe this myth, your book will disappear into the vast sea of similar books.

The trick is that you need to stand out long enough for Amazon's own marketing machine to recognize you. Once Amazon believes your book is worthy of its effort, then Amazon will work to promote you. Between the two of you, the sales of your book will improve and you'll have a shot at becoming a best seller. At least until you slip beneath Amazon's radar again.

But how do you stand out and get Amazon to recognize you over the long term?

The answer is to market your book. Yes – you. There are a number of ways to market your book. You can do promotions through Amazon (either free or the countdown). You can spend time on forums and blogs. You can use other social media such as Twitter and Facebook. You can even advertise on Facebook or LinkedIn (or Google). Ultimately, the goal is to sell enough books that Amazon realizes that it is worth spending its own time and money promoting your book.

Myth Number 6: Set it and walk away, money is generated forever

In many ways this is a variation on Myth 5: Amazon will do all your marketing for you. Many of the internet-marketing gurus suggest that you simply have to write (or buy) your book, create a cover, upload the book, and then sit back and collect the money.

Unfortunately, it doesn't work that way. As we stated under Myth 5, you need to market your book in order for Amazon to take over and start marketing it for you. Not only that but whatever you do, you will need to monitor and renew your marketing periodically.

Amazon sales take place through four main areas: the categories, the lists, the suggestions, and search. The categories are on the left side of the screen. They are how people find books when they know the topic but not which books are available. Similar to the categories are the lists. At one time the only lists were best sellers and new. However, now there are a number of other lists such as deals, picks, singles, and so forth. Each of these exist to help your readers find books they want to buy. Suggestions are the books that Amazon recommends to you when you look at a book. For example, there are two lists of "Customers also bought". This is Amazon's version of "Would you like fries with that?"

The final method readers have of finding your book is the search. This is based on the keywords that appear on your description and in the keywords field when you created your book. It also relies on the reviews your readers leave. There is also a suggestion that Amazon will soon be using the actual text of your book to help set the keywords.

In any case, it is these keywords that give the most problems for maintenance. Unfortunately, most keywords are subject to variation in the number of times they are used. And they change over time. To get the most out of your book, and to create a long-term sales pattern, you will need to observe, change the keywords you use, and record the factors. You'll also need to test any changes you are going to make.

All books have a shelf life. After a short period, your book sales will naturally fall off. Unfortunately, to get a return on the cost of your book, you need a longer shelf life than is normal. One or two weeks or one or two months isn't going to cut it. In order to lengthen this shelf life, you need to perform periodic maintenance.

Myth Number 7: Giving away your books will get you sales

When Amazon first started KDP, the Kindle Direct Publishing platform, their focus was on creating a package of books that would drive adoption of the Kindle. Everything they did was focused on this goal. The Kindle was priced at slightly above cost. The books were priced below the ten dollar threshold (typical physical books started at the $12.95 price at the time). And the promotion technique that Amazon used was the free giveaway of books.

They knew that once you got to a point where enough people used the platform, they would make money. And free was the price point that would get them there fastest.

However, they are now there. They've reached the general acceptance point and they are now the premiere hardware on the premiere platform for reading. Although physical books still outnumber eBooks, the difference is negligible.

Amazon has now begun the slow process of moving away from free. After all, as distributors free costs them money, takes away from real sales, and doesn't contribute to the bottom line. In 2012, Amazon began to remove several of the benefits of advertising free books. In fact, if the majority of your clickthroughs to their site bought only a free book, they wouldn't pay you for the paid books you sent them. They also removed the effect that free books had on the all-important rating system. In 2013, Amazon brought out the KDP Countdown promotion tool and began to hide the free books behind a number of alternative lists. With KDP Countdown, books started at 99 cents and jumped in one dollar increments. Any sales were at the full royalty rate (70% at most) and did count towards the sales ranking.

The point is that free books have four major disadvantages. First, free doesn't give you any money. I don't want to be mercenary here, but if you want to be a writer then earning money is a key component of the profession. Otherwise, you are a hobbyist (and you'll probably stop writing after you realize the amount of work involved). In fact, giving your books out free results in less real sales for you. After all, people who might have bought your book will get it without paying money for it. Second, free giveaways draw people that aren't interested in spending money. Third, they draw your competitors. Neither of these two groups are really buyers for your non-free books. They don't want to spend money and they will do everything they can to avoid doing so. Finally, free giveaways don't help your sales ranking. Amazon uses sales ranking to prioritize search results. That's why you show up at number one on a search or number 900 on a category list or on the also bought list. Unless you show up on these lists, Amazon is not really helping you to sell your book.

There are only three good results from giveaways. The first is that you may get reviews. But only if you push hard enough inside the book. And reviews do help your rankings. The second is that a book is a good way to get people to visit your website and buy more expensive products (for example $2,000 courses). And third, it's an ego boost. Which may be important if you need the encouragement.

Chapter 4: The seven tricks of information product creation

> *"Inspiration is the windfall from hard work and focus. Muses are too unreliable to keep on the payroll."*
>
> - Helen Hanson

Creating learning content can be a frustrating task. Especially if you are intending to sell it as most internet marketers are. So far, we've shared a number of myths that make creating content harder. Especially if you believe them!

But just as there are myths that send you down the wrong path, there are some secret tricks

7 Tricks

that will help you to create your course, seminars, webinars and eBooks.

Creating learning content isn't a new phenomenon as many an internet-marketing guru would have you believe. Seminars, lectures, tutorials, workshops and their supporting material have been created for many years. Over that time, techniques and systems have been developed and refined. And tricks developed.

Of course, you could just plod along trying to create your eBooks and podcasts. But doesn't it make more sense to use some of the tricks and techniques that have been developed already?

Here are seven tricks and secrets that you can use to create your learning content easily and quickly:

1. Know your audience before you start
2. Success begins with the right system
3. Do structural polishing before the heavy work
4. Use tools that work with you not against you
5. It is easier to copy than to create

6. Poor content thieves get caught. Good ones repurpose right.
7. Use Overheads Effectively & Efficiently

Let's look at each of these in turn.

Trick Number 1: Know Your Audience Before You Start

Getting to know your audience before you speak is one of those pieces of advice that's been around the speaker's circuit for years. Hanging around the front of the house is never a waste of time. Not only do you get to network with people who have actively sought you out, but you also learn what interests them and how they think. This can then be fed into your presentation. The result is a speech that more closely meets their needs. Any time your presentation better meets their needs, it will be better received. The more it meets their needs, the better it will be received.

But how do you do it when the speech is canned?

The answer is to define your audience before you start to research your topic, before you plan what you are going to talk about and long before you ever design a course. In fact, it's one of the first things you should do -- right up there with choosing your niche and making sure it has money!

But how do you do that before you have an audience?

The answer is simple. You define the audience you want to attract. Picture your perfect customer. What are they like? What do they do? What do you like about them? What makes them your perfect customer? What are their problems? What are their fears? What are their hopes and dreams? Do you have any friends that are similar to this perfect customer. Go talk to them and bounce your ideas off them.

The more you know about your perfect customer, the closer you can get to providing exactly what will attract your perfect customer. Your advertising will reflect them. Your sales pages will reflect them. Your products will reflect them.

But first, you need to know them.

Trick Number 2: Success Begins With The Right System

Defining your customer first is part of an overall system. So is doing the structural polishing before doing the heavy work. In fact, most of the seven tricks are part of an overall system.

Creating learning content -- whether in the form of live events, webinars, podcasts, teleseminars, or eBooks -- is a process. Just like building a house or a car. Or getting ready in the morning. It's a series of good habits and good practices.

What makes it a system, however, is that it is designed to interact in an efficient and effective manner. And that it is scalable and repeatable as a result.

Unfortunately, many of the systems we've been taught don't work that way. As well most of the systems will deal only with a portion of the process. After all, marketers are comfortable with marketing, teachers with teaching and training developers with writing training. But very few people are comfortable with all of the phases of the system.

As a result, you'll probably need to pick and choose pieces from several systems to build your own business system. This isn't necessarily a bad thing as it allows you to combine the best of each. However, you need to be aware of what each system's bias is. After all, you don't want to pick a marketer to teach you product creation or a training developer to teach you marketing!

Trick Number 3: Do structural polishing before the heavy work

No one is perfect. We all make mistakes. Especially when we are working with complexity. And the more complex the product is, the more errors.

That's what polishing is all about. Fixing the errors.

In writing this is called editing and is a formalized part of the process. In performance it's called practice. And it's not really that formal a process. Although the use of video recorders has improved the feedback immensely. But no matter what you call it, polishing consists of reviewing what you have done and then correcting your mistakes.

There are two major types of mistakes. The first is structural. In writing it's found by a process called structural editing. The second type of mistake is simpler and is concerned with the finish of the product. Think of blemishes on wood furniture. In writing, this is called copyediting and it deals with grammar, spelling, and sentence structure.

But whatever you call it, there are two types and they both need to be done. The trick is they need to be done at different times.

Copy or finish editing needs to be done after the product is finished. After all, you're checking to make sure that there were no mistakes in the details.

Traditionally, structural editing has been done at the end as well. In fact, usually the two types of editing are done at the same time. This is a mistake! And it's the major source of inefficiency. If you wait until the end you need to rework all of the tasks over again.

Structural editing can actually be done as soon as the structure is determined. If you are following a good learning content creation system that means it can be done as soon as the course is designed. That is before it has been written and fleshed out and while it's still in an outline form. In other words, while it is still easy to make structural changes.

By doing the structural editing as early as possible you are able to make the corrections easily and quickly. That saves you time and money over doing it after the structure has been fleshed out and finished. Waiting to the end costs you. If you find a mistake, not only will you have to correct the mistake, but you'll have to correct all the transitions and summaries that relate to the area being fixed. That normally involves a lot of work. Sometimes more than writing it the first time!

Trick Number 4: Use tools that work with you not against you

Most of us learned a basic system to create learning content while we were in school. We just happened to call the learning content essays. If you can remember that far back, you'll recognize the outlining system. (It's okay; we're allowed to make old jokes. We earned these grey hairs honestly! And no, Glen's other name isn't Santa!)

The outlining system required you to make a list of the topics you were going to write about. You then put the list in order and began to write.

For small articles, the outlining system is fine. But for small articles just about anything will work including stream of consciousness!

It's in the larger pieces that the systems break down. And learning content which is eBook length or longer is a large piece! And outlining just isn't good enough. Even if you hide it in an overlay of stepwise refinement. (Sorry, technical description of what the "Choose 15 topics, then pick ten, then choose 10 subtopics for those seven then ..." school of writing is actually doing).

For larger learning content pieces, you need a set of tools that will help you to recall, organize, and structure ideas. Three tasks that the mind is very good at -- if done one at a time. But terrible at if you try to do them all at once. To get the most from your brain means you need a set of what are known as structured cognitive tools.

Cognitive tools are tools that work with the mind and the way people think (rather than against it). But cognitive tools only help you recall or organize data. Structured tools help you to take the data and create information from it -- to organize, synthesize and structure the data into information. Structured cognitive tools combine elements of both. They assist in the recall and organization of data but they also provide a structure around the display of that data. That structure effectively transforms your data into information. Essentially your tool is tricking the mind into performing several tasks at once by providing the structure.

The alternative is a tool that does one half of the process, another tool to do the other half and having to do each piece in separate steps. Or not having a tool at all which is the worst case of all for learning content.

Trick Number 5: It's Easier To Copy Than To Create

This is the source of the repurposing myth. You know the one that says, "Do it once as a video, and then create an audio and an eBook from the result."

It's also one of the sources of efficiency in our system.

The truth is that it is easier to copy than it is to create. It's also much faster. However, the trick is in knowing when to copy and what to copy. And there are two versions (which is why there are two similar tricks). In this trick, we're really talking about creating new products from a higher level.

For example, it's much easier to create a topic map first. This map contains all the information you've gleaned from researching your topic. Its purpose is to record the information, organize it, and help you to synthesize it.

When creating your content map, it is much easier to copy information and the points you want to make from the topic map. This is true even if you are using a detailed outline rather than our system.

As you begin to create other products in the same topic or niche, this becomes more apparent. Now you can copy whole parts of the other content maps as well as from the topic map. Even so, you still want to work from the topic map. Why? Because the topic map should include the latest concepts and understandings. The content maps will have the understanding that you had of the topic when you created the product. And we all learn as we teach, don't we?

Trick Number 6: Poor content thieves get caught. Good ones repurpose right.

So why does the advice that marketing consultants give you fail? We're suggesting copying as much as they are.

The answer is in what, how and when.

Many consultants -- usually the ones selling PLR products -- suggest starting from a PLR product and then tweaking it appropriately. There are two terms for that. The first is plagiarism and the second is intellectual property theft. Even if you think you own the rights you actually don't. Sorry. Someone stole an idea from a different legal basis and forgot to check if it could translate.

"But I paid for the rights!"

Doesn't matter. All that means is the owner is unlikely to come back at you. While that is important it isn't the most important. What really matters is if the customer spots the plagiarism. And they will.

So good advice always starts with using your own material.

Much of the advice says start with recording a video, and then copy that into an audio and then transcribe that into an eBook.

And that's where the first mistakes in repurposing occur.

What is being suggested there is both that you cross media, and that you can simply copy without reworking. In fact, neither of those suggestions is correct.

There are four main rules to repurposing correctly.

When you are repurposing from one media to another, you almost always are better to start with new content maps. In other words, copy from the topic map, and existing content maps and then create a new content map. The reason for this is that you may need to add other information and techniques when converting content from one media to another. As well, it is sometimes easier to write it over from the beginning than it is to try to correct it. Which is why structural correcting is called a rewrite in writers and editors lingo.

But whether you start from a new content map or an existing product, always convert from the more complex to the simpler.

You are always going to need to add material when repurposing but creating large, complex pieces is actually easier than creating a series of small, simple pieces. The reason is that for the large piece you only need to design it once. With a series of small pieces, you need to design each piece separately. In addition, you will often find yourself duplicating content. If you then recombine the content, you will need to do a structural edit (aka a rewrite) in order to remove the duplications in the body of the piece.

In addition, you almost always need to add material regardless of the direction. This material is typically introduction, conclusion or transition rather than body. It's always easier to add introductions, conclusions to simple pieces than to complex pieces.

In addition, simple pieces don't usually require transitions. Complex pieces do.

The final rule is to determine when to use repurposing strategically. For example, if you are designing a course to be given live, on video (webinar), on audio, as an eBook and a set of articles you are better to include that in the initial design. Why? Because some learning actions work well in a live environment but work poorly in recordings. Questions are the most obvious example. Similarly, you may want to encourage note taking in a recording but not in a live environment. Videos and audios tend to be more summarized than a live event or a book. And so on. By designing all your content at the same time, you can identify what extras you will need for each and what compromises you will need. And whether you are willing to compromise at all.

The second mistake can be found in the recommendation to use PLR or private label rights. Whenever you are repurposing products you need to consider the legal ramifications. Generally speaking repurposing content you have only bought rights to should be avoided. Unfortunately, people sometimes sell things they don't have the legal ability to sell. Even though they own it, they may not be legally allowed to sell it.

Even worse in some ways is repurposing content you don't own. While we all do that, there is a difference between research and plagiarism. The biggest difference is that research is rewarded and plagiarism is punished. Don't cross the line.

So if complex to simple is the best way to go, why do the myths say write simple articles then combine them? It's simple. Most people who are starting out have a problem writing even the simplest of articles. By recommending that they start with writing the simple bits (which new training developers have a chance of finishing) and then combining that, there is a greater chance of finishing the complex work. And more importantly not scaring off a prospective customer for the gurus.

Trick Number 7: Use Overheads Effectively & Efficiently

For those of you who aren't as old as I am, an overhead was a generic term for any slide that

7 Tricks

showed behind and above the speaker as they spoke. They have been replaced almost universally by Microsoft's PowerPoint or one of its competitors. Preparing an overhead was hard work and quite expensive. They were also hard to change. As a result you wanted to use as few of them as possible. And you learned to talk a lot and write very little.

One of the biggest mistakes that new users of overheads make is that they try to cram too much on each page. Either they go into too much detail or they cover too much ground on each slide. Slides fill up with so much information that people start reading the slide and ignoring the speaker.

In fact, each slide should contain only three to five points. Talking about each point on a slide would last about 1 to 2 minutes meaning the slide lasted about 5 minutes. In one minute you can say between 80 and 160 useful words. Which is about one paragraph or half a page of writing.

More modern techniques, based on the extensive use of PowerPoint, have recommended 1 point per slide with each slide lasting 20 seconds to

1 minute plus the transition. But this is really more suitable for executive briefings and marketing efforts. Frankly it is too fast for learning and needs to be 2 to 3 times slower.

With a film, you want the editing to be fast and choppy if it is entertainment. The speed and flashing images keep you focused and enjoying. However, you need a film to be slower paced in its editing if you are trying to learn from it. Fast and choppy might entertain, but it makes absorbing information difficult. Presentations and overheads work the same way.

In any case, if we use the detailed outline technique or the concept map, each point on the map corresponds to a point on the overhead. In other words, 1 to 2 minutes of speaking and 100 words or 1 paragraph.

So when you present or write, you can use the outline or concept map as if it were an overhead or PowerPoint presentation. And vice versa. Just talk (or write) to each point for about 1 to 2 minutes. If you're writing at the end of 70 points

7 Tricks

you'll have roughly 28 pages. If you're recording you'll have 1-1/2 hours of video or audio.

Chapter 5: The benefits of an information product creation system and why your business is at risk without one

> *"The time to begin writing an article is when you have finished it to your satisfaction. By that time you begin to clearly and logically perceive what it is you really want to say."*
>
> - Samuel Clements (Mark Twain)

You may call your business "Internet Marketing", "Coaching for Success", "Online Training", "Business Consulting", "ePublishing", or any of a hundred similar names - the name doesn't matter. If you create electronic materials that advise others on how to do what they do better, then you need a reliable and effective way of producing those materials. And your system had better focus on creating products that are well organized, consistently readable (absorbable), current, and of value to your audience.

Why Use a System?

The worst process to follow is no process (A.K.A. "just wing it"). For each new information product, you do a little of this and a little of that until you are happy with the results. Changes of direction - and re-writes - are a common feature of this approach. This constant redoing of work wastes your time and creativity.

Also, you always need to provide value to your audience. This can often get lost in this unstructured environment. The result is that end up writing for you, not for them.

Using this kind of haphazard, spur of the moment process, means some of your products may be great, some so-so, and some will disappoint. Regular clients will see the inconsistency and view it as poor performance and a good reason to look elsewhere (say goodbye to some of your most loyal clients).

A good system for information product creation will ensure that your work always results in a quality product, well organized, and focused around the needs of your target audience. In addition, with a good system, you follow the same process every time. It is familiar and consistent – you always know what you are going to do at each step in the process. Major changes of direction are unlikely, and re-writes are few. And you get better (and faster) at doing each step, every time you do it. So you become both more effective and more efficient. And your information products all reflect the same look and feel – establishing your own unique "brand" and enhancing your professional status. People become familiar with how you present ideas and information, know what to expect, and learn faster as a result. This means you have happier readers and better customers.

What's in an Information Product Creation System?

A system for information product creation is a series of steps, development tasks, best practices, checkpoints, feedback loops, and confirmations that the information product development is proceeding as planned (on budget for both money and time). It is directed towards creating the right product for the client's needs. It's a quality assurance (QA) approach that says, "Nothing I publish will be of low quality, or give a negative impression to my client."

What are those steps, tasks, etc...?

We define a 9-step process to develop a new information product. The steps are listed here (and each step is described in more detail later):

1. Initial research (overview)
2. Detailed research
3. Pre-planning
4. Product Planning
5. Design
6. Structural editing
7. Content creation (writing)
8. Editing (proofing)

9. Publishing

These steps may be followed sequentially, but typically, there is some repetition and different media have different sequences in the creation/editing/publishing stages. For example, if content creation identifies questions not answered during the initial and detailed research steps, then additional research may trigger design changes, or may require re-planning. In writing, content creation is a single step as is editing. In video, creation of the script, and creation of the video are two separate steps with their own form of editing occurring between.

Researching for the New Product

Each information product you develop has a job to do – to meet the learning needs of your target audience effectively. To do this, it must be topical, timely, clear, and understandable. It must be easy to build the new understanding required. So you must understand the issues facing your target audience, what problems they have, and what ideas, guidance, and information they need to address those problems and eliminate them.

Building this "overview" of their needs ensures that you are addressing areas they are truly interested in. You should also be aware of what they are hearing from others (including myths, bad advice, and inaccurate information from so-called "gurus").

When you understand the specific needs that the new product will address (the "scope" of this particular information product), you can determine the set of topics to be presented. You already have both knowledge and experience in the general subject area. Now, you need to ensure you have an appropriate level of understanding and current knowledge on each of the specific topics chosen.

Initial research identifies the knowledge you have already. Detailed research is where you search out the additional information necessary to give the expert advice your client is looking for.

Pre-planning

Your new information product serves a need - your customer's need. But it also has a place in your overall strategy for building your business. It must work for you, or you wouldn't be writing it.

You know that you have to create a mix of products to get the results you are looking for. Typically, you will need to produce at least one free product to give away (a "freemium"). This "freemium" convinces your audience that the rest of the information you have is worth paying for. Unfortunately, this "freemium" won't actually produce any income for you. If you want to earn money from your efforts you need products that actually cost your audience money. So you will also need to be aggressively expanding the set of products you have for sale. These may include eBooks, videos, home study courses, coaching services, etc.

Within this product mix, some will be low priced (to attract attention and introduce you to new clients), some mid-priced (giving value to clients who know and trust you), and some will be high priced products (because you are recognized as a true guru – and gurus don't come cheap).

So the question is "where does this new product fit in your product mix? Once you have decided, (e.g. "this will be a mid-priced eBook"), then you can start the detailed planning that converts this vision of a product into a reality.

Planning the New Product

You now know what the new product will cover, but how will it be presented to its target audience? Is an e-book what this audience wants? Or is it better to create a video? Or maybe both? Depending on your niche, the target audience, and the product planned, you can select a preferred presentation form and media. Decisions about the size of the product (e.g. number of chapters, length of video, etc.) are made at this point. Typically, you will have a set of "templates" available that give the product the "look and feel" your company has developed as its standard offering.

The next part of planning will look at "what, who, and when." For some simple projects, this may be a simple list of tasks and timeframes. For more complex projects, a full project plan may be created showing resources to be used, the detailed tasks involved, what checkpoints, deliverables, and reviews and approvals will be required, etc. It may also build in contingency time for unexpected events. The result of this step is a detailed project plan (and costing) for the information product development. Bear in mind that this is your plan, and it is only as complicated as necessary for your needs. So don't "over plan" and turn this into a document suitable for Harlequin, Penguin Books, or Random House.

Designing the New Product

Although the form of the product, the topics to be covered, and the expected size have already been determined, many design decisions remain to be confirmed. At this point, you will be identifying the structure that will be embedded in the product.

In communicating with your audience, you need to give them not only the content (the information they need), but also an understanding of how that information will be structured, and presented to them. This is often described as "Content, Organization, and Delivery" (COD). So, in a typical information product structure, it is likely that the basic concepts will be introduced, usually sequentially, in separate sections (chapters, or video snippets), and then combined to create a more complex unit applying all the new learning.

When a new concept or technique is presented, it is usually in a three-part form consisting of an introduction (describing what is about to be presented), the body (the actual learning content), and a conclusion (summarizing, and describing how to use what you have learned). This structure within each section is often termed (IBC), and is typically how people like to receive information. So the overall information product will likely have an introduction, sections of content ("body"), and a conclusion.

Each section within the product is also likely to have its own introduction (to the particular topic under discussion), the detailed information for that section, and a conclusion. In order to help the flow of the information product, there may also be a short "bridge" to make the connection to the next section.

The other elements to consider at this time are stories and exercises. People are programmed from an early age to engage with stories. It's part of our universal culture. So telling a story of how you wrote this book or did this activity and had it blow up in your face, will help you engage with your audience. It can also be used to illustrate difficult to understand concepts. At the same time, most people learn the most by doing rather than by hearing or seeing. Especially in workshops and seminars, you will need to identify when to have them go off and practice what they have learned.

When the design is finished, the structure of the complete product is fully described. Work can start on fleshing out the sections and building the new product. But should it? We are suggesting an additional step in the process to confirm that the proposed structure is indeed the most appropriate organization and will support the best and easiest learning outcome.

Structural Editing

Traditionally, structural editing is done after all content has been developed – and a problem has been identified with the flow of the information as presented. This is late in the process, makes for re-work, and adds delays. We put this review and evaluation before content development, saving time and eliminating re-work.

In the structural edit, you examine the proposed structure and ask the following questions about the order in which information is presented, and used.

1. Do the concepts build on each other in a sequential manner?
2. Is any concept or information presented ahead of the necessary "groundwork" to support it?
3. Is the order of presentation intuitive to the proposed users of the information?
4. Does the material flow easily (e.g. are there appropriate transitions)?

If no issues are identified, then the project is ready to move into content creation. If not, the structure can be revised with low impact on the project.

Content Creation

Since the plan has identified the structure of the product in great detail, this step usually becomes a "fill in the blanks" exercise. There are headings and sub-headings identifying the content that needs to be added in each section. Note that in this context "content" is not only pure "learning content" but also includes introductions, conclusions, and bridging (transition) sections.

Many authorities suggest that content creation should be uninterrupted by any editing activities. Simply concentrate on fleshing out the ideas, making the key points, and writing clear understandable material. Don't worry about formatting, typos, or grammatical errors (since a full edit will always follow). This makes sense, particularly as more people use voice dictation rather than a keyboard.

For video and audio production, edits always have to be done after. However, the production process is actually three production processes. One for the script, one for the performance, and one for the production. Each of these has an edit (or polishing step) which needs to be performed before the next process can be performed.

Editing

Any information product will be assessed, formally or informally, on the quality of the editing by the audience. So frequent typos, or poor grammar will be seen as indicators of low quality – even if the content itself is ground-breaking and inspired! Edit cuts that sound choppy or have words trimmed in the middle will disrupt the audience. Verbal stumbling is jarring to ears raised on perfect radio and television announcers. Always make a big effort to edit out problems before any copies are published. This keeps the value in the product, and maintains a reputation for quality. This is a key point, and far too frequently an overlooked point.

Problems with poor structure can most easily be identified through issues with understanding, and in locating pertinent information. Also, finding information presented out of logical sequence. Hopefully, the structural edit has reduced or eliminated the bulk of such problems. The one thing you don't want is for your finish editor to find them. Unfortunately, they will.

Consider using an independent editor to get the best results in eliminating embarrassing edit issues. Also, consider whether the material justifies using a "fact checker" to ensure that there are no factual errors that could adversely affect your reputation.

A further editing concern has to do with how current the information presented is. Since things change very fast, consider revisiting your information products (at least) every six months to ensure that the information is still accurate and pertinent to your client's needs. If issues are found, revise and re-issue the affected documents. And advise your clients to discontinue using the old versions, and get new copies. This is also a good way to distinguish your business as conscientious and thorough.

Publishing the Product

Publishing consists of getting the product, in its final form, into the hands of its target audience. Since the form of the product is usually electronic, this means making it available to your audience in a web-friendly format (e.g. PDF, MPEG, WAV, etc.), usually delivered to their email id. In some cases, it might make sense to send a physical product (e.g. a video product on DVD, or a hard-copy version of an eBook). Make sure that any materials sent look professional (e.g. pre-printed and high-quality artwork on DVDs and packaging).

Make sure that any product the client requests (and pays for) is delivered successfully (that is: they know what to expect, they receive it exactly as promised, it is complete in every detail, and all messages to them are friendly, appropriate, and professional).

The other aspect of publishing is marketing your new information product – creating an awareness of the new product with your target audience – and making them aware of how valuable it is. How you market your products is a major part of your business strategy. It is not a simple topic and is usually the subject of significant research. Marketing this new product has to fit into that larger marketing strategy, and be appropriate for the type of product you have created.

Unfortunately, most learning creators (writers included) are not very good at marketing. After all, it runs contrary to many of our philosophies. But without marketing, our product will never reach our audience. It has to be done – and done well. Consider getting specialist advice from expert marketers, or one-on-one coaching, to ensure that your product reaches the right people.

Getting the best from your Information Product Creation System

The system for creating a quality information product presented here is a tried and tested process. Through experience, you may choose to modify the process, making it more appropriate for your context and preferred way of working. This kind of customizing and refinement is strongly encouraged. Your aim is to have a process that is efficient, repeatable, consistent, and which yields superior professional results. You want to concentrate your creative efforts on the learning experiences you are developing. The development process should not take the lion's share of those efforts.

By investing a small amount of time and effort in learning and implementing such a system, you gain the benefits described above and preserve (and hopefully enhance) your reputation as a provider of superior information products.

Chapter 6: Conclusion

We hope you found this information pertinent and useful in your business context. Please feel free to send us feedback on your experiences with this system, and any suggestions on ways we can refine it, or the description of our process provided here.

We have a number of e-books and articles describing aspects of the information product creation system in much greater detail than is found here. We have specialized documents describing the use of the system with particular media, and technologies. And we are continually refining and developing more information in this area. Feel free to contact us with your questions.

Conclusion

At http://www.LearningCreators.com you will find a free course that explains more about how we create our own learning content. It is the same process that we've used to write our books. It works and works well.

A note from the authors

We hope you enjoyed this book. We enjoy reading your mail so if you'd like to write us with any comments or things you'd like to see in coming books, you can send us mail at info@trainingnow.ca. We won't promise to include your ideas, however, we do promise to read each and every one of your emails. And we promise to at least think about your ideas. It goes without saying that compliments are always appreciated. They might even make it into print!

And speaking of comments and compliments, one of the best things you can do to show your appreciation for this or any other book, is to write a review on Amazon or wherever you bought this book. Websites like Goodreads are other places to record your opinions. Not only will you help other readers to make an informed decision but you'll help the author (or authors in this case). To submit a review of this book on Amazon go to http://www.amazon.com/dp/ B00HFWBWBC .

For More Books On Similar Topics
http://www.trainingnow.ca
For More Information On This And Related Topics
http://www.learningcreators.com/blog

TrainingNOW Books By Glen Ford

How to Write Your Own How-To EBook in 24 Hours or Less: The information products secret revealed!

How to Document a Project Plan: What you need to know to design a project management plan quickly and easily

How to Blog for Money: 9 strategies to get your blog earning money online and off

Writer's Block Demolition: Finding the time to write, keeping writing, and finish YOUR book

101 Writing Tweets: 101 tips and tweets about writing how-to books for the Kindle

As Glen Douglas

How To Build A Raised Garden Bed

With Paul Benson

101 Limericks About Public Speaking

7 Myths and Seven Tricks in Nine Steps: The truth & tricks about learning course product creation that THEY don't know

Most books are available in both Kindle and Print versions.

Who We Are

Glen Ford

Glen Ford was formerly the Chief Operating Officer/Chief Information Officer and a co-founder with VProz Inc. He is a serial entrepreneur having set up the internet training company TrainingNOW and its subsidiaries as well as providing consulting services for startups in Debt Counseling, Software and Payment Processing. He has been principal of his own project management consultancy for over 11 years. During that time he has alternated his clients between government, the big banks and small to medium companies. Prior to that he spent 10 years working for the Canadian Standards Association and 10 years alternating between large distribution and manufacturing companies. He also worked for a very successful HVAC firm. Glen is now training, writing, coaching, and consulting on project management and related entrepreneurship topics including the implementation of PMOs and methodologies. You can reach him directly through his website http://www.GlenDFord.com.

Glen is active in the business community as a member of The Project Management Institute (PMI) Lakeshore Chapter and a former training director for BNI Eagles Chapter of Business Network International (BNI). Glen is also an active supporter of charity including Scouts Canada (3rd Erin Mills Scouts). Glen holds a BSc from McMaster University in Hamilton, an MCPM from York University (Schulich), and a PMP (Project Management Professional) designation.

Paul Benson

Paul Benson is a senior partner with TrainingNOW and LearningCreators.com. Paul specializes in training development for both face-to-face (F2F) and electronic delivery (eLearning). He has been an independent IT consultant and trainer for over 20 years in Canada. His clients include major banks, insurance companies, and other financial and consulting organizations. In addition to his financial and insurance designations (C. Dip. A. F., and FLMI/M), he has a certificate in Adult Education from Brock University and is currently working on a Masters in Distance Education from Athabasca University.

TrainingNOW

TrainingNOW is a training and publishing company located in Mississauga and Burlington, Ontario, Canada. It provides specialized web hosting services for companies seeking to deliver "how to" education over the web. It also publishes and sells "how to" books and training materials in digital, print and other media. Through its subsidiaries LearningCreators and ContentCreators it provides training on how to write your own book and, provides custom training material development including books.

Glen Ford is available as a trainer, speaker, coach, or consultant. You can find more information on his courses, and services at http://GlenDFord.com

You can find more information on training courses, books, and publishing your own books at http://TrainingNOW.ca

You can find more information on creating learning content in the form of books and courses at http://www.LearningCreators.com

You can email the writers through either site.

www.ingramcontent.com/pod-product-compliance
Lightning Source LLC
Chambersburg PA
CBHW051735170526
45167CB00002B/940